Radical Healing Study Manual

Ben Diaz

Copyright 2025–Ben Diaz

All rights reserved. This book is protected by the copyright laws of the United States of America. This book may not be copied or reprinted for commercial gain or profit. The use of short quotations or occasional page copying for personal or group study is permitted and encouraged. Permission will be granted upon request. Unless otherwise indicated, all scripture quotations are taken from the *King James Version* of the Bible. Used by permission. All rights reserved.

All emphasis within Scripture quotations is the author's own. Please note that Harrison House's publishing style capitalizes certain pronouns in Scripture that refer to the Father, Son, and Holy Spirit, and may differ from some publishers' styles. Take note that the name satan and related names are not capitalized. We choose not to acknowledge him, even to the point of violating grammatical rules.

Harrison House P.O. Box 310, Shippensburg, PA 17257-0310

This book and all other Harrison House's books are available at Christian bookstores and distributors worldwide.

Reach us on the Internet: www.harrisonhouse.com.

ISBN 13 TP: 978-1-6675-1092-7

ISBN 13 eBook: 978-1-6675-1093-4

Contents

1. It All Boils Down to One Thing — 1
2. Doing the Hard Heart Work — 9
3. The Worst Day of My Life — 17
4. A Different Kind of Battle — 25
5. Praying to Uproot — 33
6. Meditating to Plant — 41
7. Declaring to Build — 47
8. A Biblical Prayer for Wholehearted Healing — 53
9. The Evidence of a Healed Heart — 61

About the Author — 69
About the Publisher — 71

Chapter 1

It All Boils Down to One Thing

"Keep your heart with all diligence, for out of it spring the issues of life." (Proverbs 4:23, NKJV)

I have the best job in the world! I take care of people from birth to death.

That's right. I've been a pastor since 2008. During that time, I have seen many ups and downs for my congregation, but there's nothing more disheartening than watching people who love God and attend church week after week fall into the same problems time and time again. I'm telling you, I've witnessed well-intended people trying so hard not to fall into the same destructive patterns over and over—so they don't get into a financial mess again, so their marriages improve, or their homes remain in peace. Sometimes the change seems to last for a little while, but they end up in that same ditch again.

I have also seen many people break free from those destructive cycles and never fall back into them again. Many of them are still in our church today, and they are a reminder to me that God's way to freedom works, that heart transformation will always trump behavior modification.

Behavior modification happens when all you have is religion—a bunch of dos and don'ts—but no relationship with the Holy Spirit. It is like makeup—it only lasts a day and needs reapplying. And like makeup that distorts or melts, religion without transformation starts looking creepy and fake. On the other hand, heart transformation is permanent and results in effortless behavioral change that aligns with the new man inside. Religion demands change on the outside, but without relationship, it has no power.

So, let me ask you this: How many times have you tried all the spiritual things—prayer, church, declarations, conferences—but still feel stuck in an area of your life? If that sounds familiar, let me encourage you. You're not broken beyond repair. You may just be missing this one crucial key that unlocks real, lasting change. It all boils down to one thing: the heart.

Focus Point

"Keep your heart with all diligence, for out of it spring the issues of life." (Proverbs 4:23, NKJV)
This verse is foundational to everything discussed in this chapter. It reminds us that the heart is not just a poetic idea or emotional center. It is the wellspring of life. Everything—relationships, finances, health, peace, fulfillment—flows from it. The condition of our heart determines the condition of our life. This is why we must give it careful attention.

Main Theme

The primary spiritual focus of this chapter is the centrality of the heart in our walk with God and the outcomes of our lives. Jesus came not merely to forgive sins but to heal the brokenhearted, restore wholeness, and bring abundant life. As believers, many of us know the Word, speak the promises, and attend church faithfully, yet we remain in cycles of defeat because our hearts have not been transformed. True change doesn't begin with striving but with surrendering our hearts to the healing work of the Holy Spirit. When our heart beliefs are aligned with God's truth, transformation flows naturally.

"Heart transformation is the starting point of every lasting breakthrough."

Key Scriptures

- *"Guard your heart above all else, for it determines the course of your life." (Proverbs 4:23, NLT)*
- *"Hope deferred makes the heart sick, but a dream fulfilled is a tree of life." (Proverbs 13:12, NLT)*
- *"He has sent Me to heal the brokenhearted, to proclaim liberty to the captives..." (Luke 4:18, NKJV)*

Key Points

- **It All Starts with the Heart** The heart is the source of everything in life. Every issue—whether good or bad—flows from what we truly believe in our hearts.
- **Behavior Modification vs. Heart Transformation** Trying to change behaviors without healing the heart leads to temporary results. Transformation comes when our hearts are renewed by God.
- **Cognitive Dissonance Sabotages Breakthrough** When we know the truth in our heads but believe a lie in our hearts, we experience an internal conflict that blocks our growth.
- **The Meaning We Assign Matters** The stories we tell ourselves in response to pain become belief systems. Wrong meanings lead to wrong beliefs, which shape our experiences.
- **Application Is the Missing Piece** Revelation is not enough. It must be applied. Without applying what we learn, we accumulate knowledge but see no transformation.
- **Testimony Is Revelation in Action** When we apply God's Word and see it work, it becomes a testimony that reinforces our heart beliefs in powerful ways.
- **Sozo Means Wholeness, Not Just Salvation** The Greek word for salvation includes healing, deliverance, and restoration. Jesus didn't just save our spirits—He came to make us whole in every area.

Journaling Questions

Journaling allows us to uncover the buried beliefs, emotions, and wounds that may be influencing our lives. This chapter teaches that our life flows from our hearts, and journaling is a way to examine and guard that inner world. As you reflect on the questions below, take time to identify what you truly believe in your heart—not just what you know in your head. It's in these vulnerable, honest moments with the Holy Spirit that the real healing begins.

As you write your responses, you may uncover places where pain, disappointment, or wrong beliefs have taken root. Don't be afraid to admit what you find. The goal is not condemnation but freedom. The Holy Spirit will meet you in your honesty and begin the gentle work of uprooting lies and planting truth. Answering these questions is the first step toward aligning your heart with the promises of God.

Recognizing the Real Issue

What cycle have I repeatedly found myself in, even after praying and trying to change?

_____
_____
_____
_____
_____
_____
_____

Head vs. Heart

Where do I believe something in my head but feel something different in my heart?

_____
_____
_____
_____
_____
_____
_____

Assigning Meaning

What painful experience have I given the wrong meaning to, and how has that belief affected my life?

_____
_____
_____
_____
_____
_____
_____

Expired Revelation

Is there a truth I once learned but never applied, which now feels distant or powerless?

_____
_____
_____
_____
_____
_____

Desire for Wholeness

What area of my life needs healing so I can experience the abundant life Jesus promised?

_____
_____
_____
_____
_____
_____

Actionable Steps

Cultivate Awareness
Spend time each day identifying emotional reactions and tracing them back to possible heart beliefs. Ask the Holy Spirit to reveal what belief is driving that feeling.

Equip Your Heart with Truth
Choose one Bible verse that speaks directly to your current struggle and meditate on it daily. Let it speak louder than the inner voices of fear, doubt, or past pain.

Engage with Your Testimony
Recall one moment in your life when you applied God's Word and saw breakthrough. Write it out, and thank God for it. Use this testimony as fuel to believe again.

Personal Reflection

Take a moment to reflect on the condition of your heart. Are there places where you've allowed pain or disappointment to shape your beliefs? Is there an area of your life that looks nothing like the promises of God, even though you know the right verses? God is not condemning you. He is inviting you into healing, into wholeness. He is showing you that the root of the issue isn't your lack of effort—it's your heart. He wants to meet you there.

Surrender is the first step. Transformation is not about trying harder, but about surrendering deeper. Trust the Holy Spirit to begin identifying and uprooting what doesn't belong so He can plant what does. Let this be your turning point. The cycles can break. The pieces can come together. But only if you take the bold step to do the heart work, not just the hard work.

Is the life I'm living the result of beliefs rooted in truth or shaped by past pain? What fruit in my life reveals what's been planted in my heart? Am I ready to let the Holy Spirit show me the missing piece?

Closing Prayer: *Holy Spirit, I open my heart to You. I no longer want to settle for cycles of brokenness or delay. Reveal what needs to be uprooted, what needs to be healed, and what needs to be believed. Help me to apply Your truth, not just hear it. I want to walk in wholeness. I surrender my heart fully to You. Amen.*

Chapter 2

Doing the Hard Heart Work

"Keep your heart with all diligence, for out of it spring the issues of life." (Proverbs 4:23, NKJV)

I have five amazing children, and I passionately love each one of them. However, as any parent knows, loving your children does not keep you from getting frustrated. We all have our triggers. Before I was a parent, I told myself I would share everything with my kids. I was determined not to be the, "That's mine, don't touch that!" kind of dad. That all changed when my son began to play with my tools and leave them scattered in the garage. He's a really creative kid who loves to build, but many times, he takes apart or even breaks things before trying to build. This became a habit for him, and after a long day's work, I would arrive home tired and seeing the tools all over the house would send me into a tailspin. I would raise my voice and say things I came to regret. The conviction would settle in during my quiet time with the Lord later in the evening. I didn't want my anger to squash my son's creativity forever! I would pray things like, "God, please give me strength and help me with my anger." I'd resist the temptation to be angry for a while, but after a few triggering instances, I'd have another outburst. So what was the real solution? Well, I can tell you it is not working harder at the problem but rather doing the heart work to remove the problem from its root.

The Holy Spirit revealed to me that the root cause for my anger was a lack of patience. I was trying to treat the symptom instead of healing the core issue. Once I realized that, I began to meditate on scriptures about patience and declare those truths over my life until they became a part of me. Anger began to fade, not by force, but because the Holy Spirit was doing a deeper work in me. I had the fruit of the Spirit already inside me—what I needed was to cultivate it. That's what this chapter is about: dealing with the roots instead of trimming weeds.

When we're stuck, we often work harder in the wrong direction. But God wants to show us a better way.

The issues in our lives—addictions, frustrations, fears—are often symptoms of deeper heart beliefs that we're not even aware of. Instead of managing those symptoms through behavior modification, we need to let God show us the root. Sometimes that root is a belief formed in childhood. Sometimes it's a lie we agreed with in pain. The good news is this: you don't have to fight a thousand battles. You only need to go to the source, and that source is your heart.

What are you spinning your wheels on today? What's that issue that keeps resurfacing no matter how hard you try to overcome it? God doesn't want to shame you—He wants to set you free. And freedom starts with slowing down, inviting the Holy Spirit into your heart, and letting Him show you what's really going on underneath the surface.

Focus Point

"Keep your heart with all diligence, for out of it spring the issues of life." (Proverbs 4:23, NKJV)

This verse reminds us that every issue in our life flows from our heart. It's not about fixing behaviors, managing emotions, or suppressing feelings. If our heart isn't healed, our life reflects it. God invites us to guard, tend, and heal our hearts because it determines the course of everything else. Your healing begins when you take a courageous step toward doing the heart work.

Main Theme

The central theme of this chapter is that transformation happens from the inside out, not the outside in. We've been trained to deal with symptoms—to medicate pain, suppress emotions, and adjust our behaviors. But God wants to deal with the root causes of our dysfunction. This chapter is about recognizing that spiritual growth and healing begin with uncovering the hidden beliefs in our hearts. With the help of the Holy Spirit, we can uproot lies, destroy wrong patterns, and create space for God's truth to take root and grow. True transformation happens when we allow God to work on the foundation.

"Don't just modify behavior—let God transform your heart from the inside out."

Key Scriptures

- *"Keep your heart with all diligence, for out of it spring the issues of life." (Proverbs 4:23, NKJV)*
- *"Do not conform to the pattern of this world, but be transformed by the renewing of your mind." (Romans 12:2, NIV)*
- *"Some you must uproot and tear down, destroy and overthrow. Others you must build up and plant." (Jeremiah 1:10, NLT)*

Key Points

- **Symptoms Reveal the Root** Anger, addiction, and fear are often symptoms of a deeper issue. The real work isn't in suppressing them but discovering their root.
- **Heart Work Over Hard Work** Spinning your wheels with more effort won't lead to breakthrough. It's heart work—not more effort—that leads to lasting change.
- **The Danger of Distraction** The enemy keeps us distracted and busy trimming weeds so we don't deal with the deeper issues. Heart work requires slowing down and being still with God.
- **Foundations Must Be Rebuilt** Like the Leaning Tower of Pisa, building on a broken foundation creates long-term instability. Uprooting and rebuilding is essential for sustained growth.
- **Preparation Comes Before Growth** Before God can build and plant in your life, He must uproot, destroy, and tear down everything opposing His truth.
- **God Restores What You Let Him Uproot** When we surrender to the demo process, God promises to replant, restore, and faithfully build something far better in its place.
- **Transformation Begins with Honesty** Freedom starts when we're honest with ourselves and God. Avoiding heart work only delays the breakthrough we desperately need.

Journaling Questions

Journaling is an act of courage. It slows us down and opens a conversation with God about what's really going on inside. In this chapter, we explore how many of the issues we battle aren't the main issue—they're symptoms. As you take time to reflect, ask the Holy Spirit to show you what belief or experience is at the root of the struggle. You're not just looking for answers; you're looking for truth that heals.

These journaling questions will help you uncover what might be hiding beneath the surface. You may find a lie you believed in childhood, a memory that caused shame, or a wound that hasn't been addressed. Don't rush this time. The Holy Spirit is gentle but thorough, and He will guide you into freedom as you write with honesty and expectation.

Recurring Frustrations

What behaviors or struggles have I tried to change repeatedly without lasting success?

_____
_____
_____
_____
_____
_____
_____

Digging Deeper

When I examine these struggles, what belief or feeling seems to lie underneath?

_____
_____
_____
_____
_____
_____
_____

Exposing the Foundation

Have I been trying to build something new (in life or faith) on a cracked or unstable foundation?

_____
_____
_____
_____
_____
_____

Surrendering to Demo Day

What do I sense God is asking me to uproot, tear down, or surrender in this season?

_____
_____
_____
_____
_____
_____

Choosing Heart Work

Am I willing to slow down and let the Holy Spirit do the heart work, even if it feels uncomfortable?

_____
_____
_____
_____
_____
_____

Actionable Steps

Cultivate Honesty
Create space each day to ask, "What am I really feeling?" and "What do I believe about this?" Honesty is the doorway to healing.

Equip with Scripture
Find one verse that directly confronts the root belief God has revealed. Write it down and speak it aloud daily as a declaration of truth.

Engage in Uprooting
Take time in prayer to invite the Holy Spirit to uproot what's not of Him. Visualize Him removing old roots and preparing the soil of your heart for new growth.

Personal Reflection

What part of your life feels like it's been stuck or spinning in circles? That area might be God's invitation to do heart work. He's not waiting for you to try harder—He's waiting for you to surrender deeper. As you reflect, ask yourself whether you've truly allowed the Holy Spirit access to the roots beneath the struggle. Transformation begins when we give God the permission to touch the things we've buried.

Growth isn't always glamorous. Before we build something new, we must first clear the ground. That means letting go of control, facing discomfort, and doing the work no one else sees. But what God plants in a yielded heart will grow into something beautiful and lasting. You don't have to live in frustration any longer. You were made to flourish.

What needs to be uprooted before I can be planted? What heart belief is keeping me in cycles of pain or frustration? Am I ready to let the Holy Spirit dig deeper and start fresh?

_____
_____
_____
_____
_____
_____
_____

Closing Prayer: *Father, I surrender my heart to You. Uproot every belief, every fear, and every lie that's keeping me bound. Tear down what was not built by You and prepare the soil of my heart for Your truth. I don't want to stay stuck. I choose to trust You with my healing and with my foundation. Do the work only You can do. Amen.*

Chapter 3

The Worst Day of My Life

"These things I have spoken to you, that in Me you may have peace. In the world you will have tribulation; but be of good cheer, I have overcome the world." (John 16:33, NKJV)

One beautiful Saturday morning in April of 2021, my friend Carlos and his son Jordan invited me to ride dirt bikes with them in the desert. For months, we had tried to plan this trip, and our schedules finally coincided. I'm not a very consistent rider, but I'll carefully hop on a motorcycle a handful of times a year. However, by no means am I the type to push the limits or take unnecessary risks. So, on this particular expedition, I let Jordan take the lead. He and Carlos had been on this trail many times, and I was the newbie. I was not about to venture off on my own path! We headed off to a lake about 90 minutes away, gliding over firm ground, rocky soil, sandy terrain, and loose gravel. We went up and down steep hills, and I wasn't having any issues. I felt confident but remained cautious.

Suddenly, we came to a steep hill—the kind you have to commit to once you start. If you stop halfway, your bike will fall on you. As I followed Jordan down, he veered to the left side of the trail. I stayed on the right. Big mistake. My side dropped faster. Two feet. Four feet. Six feet. My front tire hit the ground and the handlebars twisted. I was launched off a 20-foot drop. My legs tangled with the bike, and I hit the ground hard. The pressure forced my knee into a 90-degree angle. I heard a loud crack. Right next to me was a rusty steel rebar. If I'd landed one foot to the right, I would have been impaled.

In an instant, everything changed. The doctors confirmed I had torn every tendon and ligament in my leg except for the ACL. I was hanging on by skin and muscle. That injury became the worst trauma of my life—and not just physically. In the days and weeks to come, I realized that pain has a way of exposing things we didn't even know were broken. My heart, my faith, my emotions—they all needed healing too.

Maybe you've been there. One moment life is good. The next, everything feels like it's crumbling. You might have the Word in your heart and a history with God, but still find yourself in a place where you're wondering, "Why didn't it work this time?" I want to encourage you: God does not waste pain. He uses it to uncover what needs healing, and He walks with us through every moment of that healing process.

Focus Point

"These things I have spoken to you, that in Me you may have peace. In the world you will have tribulation; but be of good cheer, I have overcome the world." (John 16:33, NKJV)

This verse is a lifeline in seasons of crisis. Jesus doesn't sugarcoat the reality of hardship—He promises it. But He also promises something greater: His peace. We're not guaranteed a pain-free life, but we are guaranteed His overcoming presence. That truth sustains us when the worst day of your life arrives.

Main Theme

The focus of this chapter is the unavoidable reality of pain and how God uses those painful moments to lead us deeper into healing and revelation. It's about how trauma and crisis—though never desired—can become the doorway to transformation. When we let God into the brokenness, He not only heals, He rebuilds stronger. This chapter is an invitation to surrender our suffering and invite God to do a work that goes far beyond the physical. It's the beginning of a deeper trust that only comes through walking through pain with Him.

"Your pain may surprise you, but it will never surprise God—and He can use it to start the greatest healing of your life."

Key Scriptures

- *"He heals the brokenhearted and binds up their wounds." (Psalm 147:3, NKJV)*
- *"My grace is sufficient for you, for My strength is made perfect in weakness." (2 Corinthians 12:9, NKJV)*

- *"Though I walk through the valley of the shadow of death, I will fear no evil; for You are with me." (Psalm 23:4, NKJV)*

Key Points

- **Crisis Can Come Suddenly** One moment can shift everything. But the God who is with you on the mountaintop is also with you in the valley.
- **Pain Exposes What's Hidden** The accident revealed things in my heart I hadn't realized needed healing. Physical pain triggered emotional and spiritual reflection.
- **Healing Is Holistic** True healing isn't just physical. God wants to restore our emotions, faith, and identity too.
- **Trauma Creates Entry Points** Pain can open doors to fear, disappointment, and hopelessness. But it can also open the door to deeper trust in God.
- **The Most Important Work Is Heart Work** As my friend Chad told me, "It's going to be a lot of hard work, but the most important work is the heart work."
- **You Can Love God and Still Struggle** Faith doesn't make you immune to hardship. Even pastors and leaders face seasons of deep pain and need healing.
- **God Uses Everything** No pain is wasted. God works through the worst days to bring about transformation and revelation we would have never reached otherwise.

Journaling Questions

Journaling during a season of pain can be one of the most healing things you can do. This chapter invites us to stop numbing or avoiding our pain and instead let God meet us there. When you write honestly, it gives the Holy Spirit room to speak and minister to those raw places inside you. He already knows what's there. The journal simply gives you the courage to face it with Him.

Reflect deeply. Where have you questioned God in your crisis? What fears entered when life spun out of control? What beliefs were shaken? These questions aren't signs of doubt—they're invitations to go deeper. Your honesty will become the soil for your healing.

The Impact of Crisis

What was a moment or season in my life where everything suddenly changed? How did I respond?

_____
_____
_____
_____
_____
_____
_____

What Pain Revealed

What did that pain expose about my heart, beliefs, or fears?

_____
_____
_____
_____
_____
_____

Beyond the Physical

Have I been focusing only on physical or external healing while neglecting what's going on in my heart?

_____
_____
_____
_____
_____
_____

Letting God In

Have I invited God into the most painful part of my story, or have I shut Him out?

_____
_____
_____
_____
_____
_____

Choosing Trust Again

What would it look like for me to trust God again, even in the areas that hurt the most?

_____
_____
_____
_____
_____
_____

Actionable Steps

Cultivate Surrender
Write out a prayer of surrender, even if you don't fully feel it yet. Let your heart begin to say, "God, I give You this pain."

Equip with Compassion
Be gentle with yourself. Identify one thing you would say to a friend in your situation—and say it to yourself.

Engage Your Healing
Ask God to show you one area of the heart He wants to heal through this situation. Write it down and pray into it daily this week.

Personal Reflection

There are moments that break us. And sometimes, those broken places become the very ground where God begins His greatest work. You might be walking through your own worst day—or you may still carry the weight of a past one. Know this: you are not alone. Jesus said we would face trouble in this world, but He also said He has overcome it. And that includes your pain.

Pain is never the end of your story. It's often the doorway to discovering who God really is and who you are in Him. Don't rush past the healing process. Lean into it. Let Him walk you through every layer. You are not weak for needing healing. You are wise for seeking it.

Have I allowed pain to write my story, or am I letting God rewrite it? What beauty might be waiting on the other side of this pain? Am I willing to walk with God through every layer, even the ones I've avoided?

Closing Prayer: *Father, I bring You my pain. I don't want to ignore it or numb it any longer. I invite You into the places where it hurts the most. Thank You for never leaving me—even when I don't understand. Use this moment to begin something new in me. Bring healing to my heart, my mind, and my soul. I trust You with the journey. Amen.*

Chapter 4

A Different Kind of Battle

"For though we walk in the flesh, we do not war according to the flesh. For the weapons of our warfare are not carnal but mighty in God for pulling down strongholds." (2 Corinthians 10:3-4, NKJV)

After my accident, I found myself alone in the house one night while my wife and kids were out. I was on the couch in a full leg cast, dealing with immense pain and feeling completely helpless. I looked around at the silence, at the things I couldn't do, and I began to cry. My body was broken, my emotions were raw, and my spirit felt shaken. In that moment, the battle wasn't physical—it was emotional and spiritual. The questions started to flood in: "Will I recover?" "Why did this happen?" "Did I fail God somehow?"

That night, I realized something crucial: not all battles are fought in the body. Some are fought in the soul, in the quiet corners of our minds where fear and lies try to take root. The enemy doesn't always come with obvious attacks. Sometimes, he whispers doubts into our fatigue, plants discouragement in our pain, and waits for us to agree with him. But God invites us to fight differently—not with fists or willpower, but with divine weapons that heal and restore from the inside out.

This was a different kind of battle. One I couldn't fight with declarations alone or push through with positivity. I needed to partner with God on a deeper level. This wasn't about asking for relief anymore; it was about waging war for my heart, my identity, and my faith. And that's exactly what God began to show me how to do.

Are you in a battle today that feels more spiritual than physical? Are you growing weary, wondering if God still hears you? If so, this chapter is for you. It's time to pick up the right weapons for a different kind of war.

Focus Point

"For though we walk in the flesh, we do not war according to the flesh. For the weapons of our warfare are not carnal but mighty in God for pulling down strongholds." (2 Corinthians 10:3-4, NKJV)

This verse reminds us that the real battlefield isn't what we see—it's what we believe. The enemy wages war in our thoughts, in our identity, and in our emotions. But God has equipped us with supernatural weapons to destroy lies, cast down fear, and uproot the strongholds that try to keep us stuck. The key is learning how to use them.

Main Theme

This chapter reveals that many of the battles we face are not external but internal—fought in the heart and mind. Emotional exhaustion, discouragement, and hopelessness are often signs of a spiritual battle. The enemy tries to wear us down subtly, but God calls us to fight with the weapons He provides: prayer, truth, meditation, and declaration. These aren't religious rituals—they're tools of divine power meant to pull down the strongholds of fear, shame, and brokenness. You are not powerless. You are fully armed for a different kind of battle.

"When the battlefield is in your mind, the Word of God becomes your sword."

Key Scriptures

- *"For the weapons of our warfare are not carnal but mighty in God for pulling down strongholds." (2 Corinthians 10:4, NKJV)*
- *"Be strong in the Lord and in the power of His might. Put on the whole armor of God." (Ephesians 6:10-11, NKJV)*
- *"You will keep him in perfect peace, whose mind is stayed on You, because he trusts in You." (Isaiah 26:3, NKJV)*

Key Points

- **A Battle Beyond the Physical** Not every struggle shows up in your body. Many are in your emotions, thoughts, and beliefs. Learn to recognize a spiritual fight.
- **Warfare in the Mind** The enemy attacks through lies, discouragement, and fear. He wants you to agree with his version of reality, not God's.
- **Weariness Is a Signal** Emotional exhaustion is often a sign that you're battling in your own strength. You were never meant to fight alone.
- **God's Weapons Are Divine** Prayer, Scripture, worship, and declarations are not religious duties—they are spiritual weapons with real power.
- **Victory Requires Agreement** Breakthrough happens when you agree with God's truth instead of the enemy's lies. Agreement determines outcome.
- **The Heart Needs Guarding** Your emotions are vulnerable during pain. Guard your heart, especially when you feel weak, confused, or disappointed.
- **Peace Is a Weapon** God's peace isn't passive. It crushes fear, silences anxiety, and steadies you in the storm. Keep your mind fixed on Him.

Journaling Questions

This chapter calls for a new kind of reflection—one that helps you recognize when you're in a spiritual battle, even if your circumstances seem normal. Journaling is how you identify the battlefield. It's where you draw the map, name the enemy, and choose your weapons. You don't need to be overwhelmed anymore. You can take your power back.

As you journal, let the Holy Spirit reveal where the enemy has been attacking you. Is it fear? Hopelessness? Insecurity? Unforgiveness? Start naming the lies you've believed. Then begin replacing them with the truth of God's Word. Victory starts with clarity—and clarity comes through reflection.

Naming the Battlefield

Where have I been feeling worn down, anxious, or discouraged? Could it be a spiritual battle?

_____
_____
_____

Recognizing the Tactic

What lie or thought has been playing on repeat in my mind lately?

_____
_____
_____
_____
_____
_____

Exposing the Agreement

Have I unintentionally agreed with a lie the enemy is trying to plant?

_____
_____
_____
_____
_____
_____

Choosing New Weapons

Which spiritual weapon (prayer, Scripture, declaration) do I need to begin using consistently in this season?

_____
_____
_____
_____
_____
_____
_____

Restoring My Peace

What truth from God's Word do I need to meditate on to experience peace again?

_____
_____
_____
_____
_____
_____

Actionable Steps

Cultivate Alertness
Start each day by asking, "What is the enemy trying to attack in me today?" Be aware and refuse to agree with lies.

Equip with the Word
Write down one scripture that confronts the lie you're battling. Read it aloud every day this week until it feels more real than the fear.

Engage with Peace
Before reacting to emotions or circumstances, pause. Ask the Holy Spirit, "Where is Your peace in this moment?" Let peace guide your response.

Personal Reflection

You may be in a battle right now that doesn't make sense on the surface. That's because it's deeper—it's spiritual. But you are not without help. God has given you the weapons. He's also given you the authority to use them. You don't need to live in fear, confusion, or fatigue. You were born for victory.

You're not called to strive. You're called to stand. In the middle of the storm, God gives you armor, a sword, and His Spirit to lead you into triumph. So today, refuse to fight with your fists. Fight with your faith. Guard your mind, fill your heart with truth, and let peace be your weapon.

What lies have I been believing about myself or my situation? Am I fighting in my own strength or with God's weapons? What would it look like to stand in peace and truth today?

Closing Prayer: *Father, I surrender every battle I've been trying to fight on my own. Open my eyes to the war in my mind, and teach me to use the weapons You've given me. Help me to cast down every lie and hold fast to Your truth. I choose peace. I choose faith. I choose to fight Your way. Amen.*

Chapter 5

Praying to Uproot

"Every plant which My heavenly Father has not planted will be uprooted." (Matthew 15:13, NKJV)

Not long after my accident, as I was still healing physically and emotionally, I began to feel overwhelmed by layers of inner pain that I didn't even know were still in me. I had already begun the journey of recognizing that the most important work is the heart work, but I needed a way to actually *do* it. One day in prayer, the Holy Spirit spoke gently but clearly: "Start here. Start with prayer. Let Me help you uproot the lies."

That was the turning point. Up until that moment, I had used prayer like a tool to get things from God—a solution for problems, a lifeline in emergencies, a connection point. But now, He was inviting me into something much deeper. Not prayer as a request list, but prayer as a divine excavation. I wasn't just praying to be heard; I was praying to be healed.

Through this process, I realized that prayer isn't just about talking—it's about uncovering. It's a safe space where God shows us what doesn't belong in our hearts anymore. And once those false beliefs, fears, or wounds are identified, we can partner with the Holy Spirit to uproot them, just like Jesus promised. Prayer became a mirror and a scalpel. It helped me identify the weeds and begin the healing process.

Maybe you've been praying, but nothing seems to change. Could it be that God is waiting to show you what's underneath the surface? Prayer is the first step to breakthrough—not because God needs convincing, but because your heart needs revealing.

Focus Point

"Every plant which My heavenly Father has not planted will be uprooted." (Matthew 15:13, NKJV)

This verse is an invitation and a promise. It tells us that God never intended for us to live with false beliefs, destructive patterns, or hidden pain. If it didn't come from Him, it doesn't have to stay. Through prayer, we come into agreement with His will to uproot what doesn't belong. This is not punishment—it's healing.

Main Theme

This chapter emphasizes prayer as the primary tool God gives us to uproot lies, trauma, and wrong heart beliefs. Prayer isn't just for comfort or communication—it's for transformation. It's the starting point for healing, the place where our hearts are examined and the lies of the enemy are brought into the light. As we pray with the Holy Spirit, He reveals the root issues beneath our pain and gently begins the process of pulling them out. This is how freedom begins: not by asking God to change everything around us, but by allowing Him to change everything inside us.

"Prayer is not about getting God's attention—it's about letting Him get to the root of your heart."

Key Scriptures

- *"Every plant which My heavenly Father has not planted will be uprooted." (Matthew 15:13, NKJV)*
- *"Search me, O God, and know my heart; try me, and know my anxieties." (Psalm 139:23, NKJV)*
- *"You do not have because you do not ask God." (James 4:2, NIV)*

Key Points

- **Prayer Reveals Hidden Roots** True prayer allows God to shine light on the inner lies and wounds we may not even be aware of.

- **God Is Not the Source of Every Seed** If something in your heart didn't originate from the Father—like fear, shame, or rejection—it must be uprooted.
- **Agreement Activates Uprooting** God will not force healing upon us. We must invite Him to remove the wrong beliefs we've agreed with.
- **Prayer Is a Two-Way Exchange** It's not just about asking—it's about listening. God reveals truth when we make space to hear.
- **Honest Prayer Unlocks Healing** Being vulnerable and raw in prayer opens the door to deeper healing. God can't heal what we won't reveal.
- **Uprooting Prepares for Planting** When lies and trauma are uprooted, space is created for truth and identity to take root.
- **Persistent Prayer Shapes Belief** As you keep praying and surrendering, your heart begins to align more with God's truth than your old patterns.

Journaling Questions

This chapter calls for deep, vulnerable prayer—not the kind filled with eloquence or perfect words, but the kind where you bring your honest heart to God. Journaling is a helpful companion to prayer because it allows you to notice patterns, document what God reveals, and follow the thread of what He's uprooting.

Think of journaling as spiritual gardening. You're asking God to show you the weeds. As He does, you write them down—not to dwell on them, but to expose them to His truth. Then you give Him permission to pull them out, one by one. This is slow, sacred work. Don't rush. Let the Holy Spirit lead.

Inviting the Uprooting

What is one belief or emotion that I sense doesn't come from God, but I've allowed it to take root?

_____
_____
_____
_____
_____

Reflecting on the Fruit

What kind of "fruit" (emotions, reactions, habits) has this false belief produced in my life?

_____
_____
_____
_____
_____
_____

Listening in Prayer

When I quiet myself in prayer, what do I sense the Holy Spirit is gently bringing to my attention?

_____
_____
_____
_____
_____

Releasing Agreement

What agreement do I need to break today—something I've believed about myself, others, or God?

_____
_____
_____
_____
_____
_____

Welcoming God's Truth

What truth do I need to invite in to replace the lie that's being uprooted?

_____
_____
_____
_____
_____

Actionable Steps

Cultivate Vulnerability
Set aside 10 minutes of quiet time to speak honestly with God—no filters, no performance. Just your heart.

Equip Your Prayer Life
Keep a prayer journal specifically for the purpose of uprooting. Write down what God shows you and the truths He gives in exchange.

Engage with Daily Surrender
Each morning, pray this simple line: "God, uproot anything in me that You didn't plant." Repeat it until your heart begins to yield.

Personal Reflection

There are things in your heart that God never planted. Some of them came from trauma. Some came from culture. Others were passed down through generations. But now, He's inviting you to let Him remove what's hurting you. The healing process begins when you stop hiding the weeds and start inviting the Gardener in.

You were never meant to carry false beliefs, shame, or fear. Prayer is the tool that unlocks your freedom. Don't settle for surface-level faith. Go deep with God. Let Him search, uproot, and restore. He's not mad at you—He's moving toward you with love.

What have I allowed to grow in my heart that's not from God? Am I willing to let Him pull it out, even if it's painful? What kind of life could I live if my heart was truly free?

Closing Prayer: *Father, I invite You to search my heart. Show me what doesn't belong. Uproot every lie, every fear, every false belief that's keeping me stuck. I choose to break agreement with anything You didn't plant in me. Plant Your truth deep in my soul. I trust You with the process. In Jesus' name, amen.*

Chapter 6

Meditating to Plant

"But his delight is in the law of the Lord, and in His law he meditates day and night. He shall be like a tree planted by the rivers of water, that brings forth its fruit in its season, whose leaf also shall not wither; and whatever he does shall prosper." (Psalm 1:2-3, NKJV)

Once I realized how prayer could uproot the lies that had been ruling my heart, I discovered another crucial piece of the healing journey—*planting* truth. I remember one morning sitting quietly in my office with my Bible open. I wasn't rushing to get through a chapter or complete a plan. I was simply meditating on one verse. And in that stillness, I heard the Lord say, "Now that we've uprooted the lies, it's time to plant the truth."

That moment shifted my mindset. I had spent years reading the Bible, but this was different. This wasn't about gaining information—it was about transformation. Meditation wasn't a mental exercise; it was a spiritual discipline. As I began to meditate on God's Word—slowly, repeatedly, and prayerfully—I noticed something happening. Truth began to take root in me. I wasn't just trying to believe something. I *became* someone new.

Meditation is where the Word goes from head knowledge to heart revelation. It's where truth gets planted so deeply that it starts producing fruit naturally. In those moments of silent focus and listening, God redefines our identity, rewrites our beliefs, and renews our minds. What was once a battlefield becomes a garden.

So if prayer uproots, meditation plants. If you want to walk in lasting freedom, you can't stop at removing lies. You must replace them with truth that runs deep. Meditation is the way.

Focus Point

"But his delight is in the law of the Lord, and in His law he meditates day and night. He shall be like a tree planted by the rivers of water..." (Psalm 1:2–3, NKJV)

This scripture captures the transformative power of meditation. The one who meditates on God's Word becomes rooted, steady, and fruitful. This isn't about reading a verse once—it's about soaking in it until it becomes a part of you. Meditation allows the truth to shape your thoughts, emotions, and identity, producing strength and spiritual maturity.

Main Theme

This chapter unveils meditation as the God-ordained method for planting truth deep within our hearts. After lies are uprooted, our hearts become fertile ground, ready for new seeds. But those seeds—God's words and promises—only grow when we linger with them. Meditation is how we turn revelation into transformation. It's how we shift from *knowing* a truth to *becoming* it. In the garden of your heart, meditation is the watering process. As you delight in God's Word and give it space to speak, you'll begin to see fruit: peace, strength, identity, and prosperity.

Meditation turns God's truth from information into transformation."

Key Scriptures

- *"But his delight is in the law of the Lord, and in His law he meditates day and night." (Psalm 1:2, NKJV)*
- *"This Book of the Law shall not depart from your mouth, but you shall meditate in it day and night... for then you will make your way prosperous, and then you will have good success." (Joshua 1:8, NKJV)*
- *"Let the word of Christ dwell in you richly in all wisdom..." (Colossians 3:16, NKJV)*

Key Points

- **Meditation Plants the Word** When you meditate on Scripture, it becomes deeply rooted in your heart and starts to shape your inner world.

- **Truth Needs Time to Grow** Like a seed, God's Word takes time to take root and bear fruit. Meditation gives it the space and nourishment it needs.
- **From Head to Heart** Information changes nothing without transformation. Meditation moves truth from your head to your heart.
- **Identity Is Rewritten in Meditation** As you meditate, you begin to see yourself through God's eyes, replacing old labels with divine identity.
- **Meditation Produces Stability** The one who meditates is like a tree—planted, nourished, and unshakable. This is how we weather emotional storms.
- **Delight Leads to Depth** The more you delight in God's Word, the deeper your roots grow. Joy and consistency go hand in hand.
- **Meditation Is a Spiritual Discipline** It requires intentional time, focus, and repetition. But the fruit it produces makes the effort worth it.

Journaling Questions

This chapter highlights the vital role of meditation in the healing process. While prayer reveals what must be removed, meditation reveals what must be restored. Journaling becomes a helpful companion as you begin to write down verses that speak directly to your identity, pain, or healing. As you journal, you're not just documenting thoughts—you're cultivating the soil for spiritual growth.

Let your journal become a garden log. Track what you're planting, how it's growing, and what God is speaking through His Word. Write out the same verse each day if needed. Let it sink in. Listen to how the Holy Spirit personalizes the Scripture for your journey. Transformation happens not just when we read the Word—but when the Word reads us.

Sowing the Seed

What is one Scripture that speaks directly to a lie I recently uprooted?

_____
_____
_____
_____
_____
_____
_____

Delighting in the Word

What does it look like for me to truly delight in God's Word, rather than just study it?

_____
_____
_____
_____
_____

Rooting My Identity

What truth do I want to take root in my identity this week?

_____
_____
_____
_____
_____
_____
_____

Slow Growth

Have I been impatient in the transformation process? What does God want to remind me about the power of slow, steady growth?

_____
_____
_____
_____
_____
_____

Becoming the Tree

What fruit do I want to see in my life as a result of meditating on God's Word?

_____
_____
_____
_____
_____

Actionable Steps

Cultivate Consistency
Pick one Scripture for the week. Read it every morning and night. Let it become a part of you.

Equip Your Environment
Write the verse on a notecard and place it somewhere visible—your mirror, dashboard, or desk. Create an atmosphere where truth stays in front of you.

Engage with Depth
Take five minutes each day to speak the verse out loud, reflect on each word, and ask the Holy Spirit to reveal something new.

Personal Reflection

Healing doesn't just mean clearing out pain—it means replacing it with something beautiful and lasting. God wants His truth to take deep root in your heart, so it can bear fruit that blesses every part of your life. Meditation is how you partner with Him to make that happen.

Don't underestimate the power of one verse planted deeply. That verse can change your mind, your emotions, and your destiny. As you slow down and soak in Scripture, you're inviting God to redefine you from the inside out. This is how transformation becomes permanent.

What truth do I need to let settle deep into my heart? Am I willing to make room for it daily through meditation? How would my life change if I became deeply rooted in God's Word?

Closing Prayer: *Father, thank You for the gift of Your Word. Help me to meditate on it day and night, to delight in it, and to plant it deeply in my heart. Let truth grow strong in me. Let it transform my thoughts, renew my identity, and produce lasting fruit in my life. In Jesus' name, amen.*

Chapter 7

Declaring to Build

"Death and life are in the power of the tongue, and those who love it will eat its fruit." (Proverbs 18:21, NKJV)

There was a time when I didn't realize the power of my own words. I used to speak out of emotion, circumstance, or habit without thinking about the effect it had on my heart and life. But one day, the Lord began to convict me of the things I was saying—not to shame me, but to awaken me. He showed me that my words were either building something or tearing something down. And if I wanted to live in wholeness, I couldn't stay passive about what I was saying.

I began to see that declaring God's truth was a key part of healing. Just as prayer uproots and meditation plants, declaration builds. Speaking God's Word aloud, over myself, aligned my heart with heaven. It wasn't just about reciting verses—it was about using my God-given authority to shape the atmosphere of my life. My declarations became spiritual blueprints, constructing a life rooted in truth.

As I continued this practice, I noticed that things started to shift—internally and externally. My mind became clearer. My emotions steadied. I felt more anchored in identity. It didn't happen overnight, but with each declaration, I was participating in the rebuilding of my soul. God had given me a voice, not just to communicate but to co-create.

You have the same invitation. Your words matter. And when they echo the Word of God, they carry power to build what hell tried to tear down. Don't underestimate what happens when you open your mouth in agreement with heaven.

Focus Point

"Death and life are in the power of the tongue, and those who love it will eat its fruit." (Proverbs 18:21, NKJV)

This verse highlights a foundational truth: your words have creative power. What you speak determines the atmosphere you live in. When you declare God's Word, you're not just saying nice things—you're shaping reality. The fruit of your words becomes the experience of your life. Choose them wisely, and declare life.

Main Theme

This chapter focuses on the power of declaration in the healing process. Once lies are uprooted through prayer and truth is planted through meditation, we begin to reinforce that truth by speaking it. Declaration is not mindless repetition—it's intentional agreement with what God has said. Every time we speak His Word, we're building strength, structure, and security into our hearts. Declarations aren't just tools for encouragement; they are instruments of construction. As we declare what God says about us, our healing, our identity, and our destiny, we are actively participating in the rebuilding of our lives.

"When you declare God's truth, you're not pretending something is real—you're partnering with what is already true in heaven."

Key Scriptures

- *"Death and life are in the power of the tongue, and those who love it will eat its fruit." (Proverbs 18:21, NKJV)*
- *"Let the weak say, 'I am strong.'" (Joel 3:10, NKJV)*
- *"I believed, and therefore I spoke." (2 Corinthians 4:13, NKJV)*

Key Points

- ***Key Points***
- **Declaration Builds Identity** Speaking God's truth over yourself helps rewire old patterns and reinforce your true identity in Christ.

- **Words Are Construction Tools** Every declaration lays a brick in the spiritual structure of your life. You are building or breaking with your words.
- **Your Voice Is a Weapon** Declaring God's Word aloud pushes back darkness and ushers in light. It's a powerful act of spiritual warfare.
- **Faith Speaks** Belief isn't silent. When you believe God's Word, you speak it. Declaration is evidence of faith.
- **Daily Declarations Reinforce Healing** Consistency matters. The more you declare truth, the more your heart aligns with it.
- **Your Words Create Your Atmosphere** The tone of your life will often reflect the tone of your tongue. Speak life and watch your world shift.
- **Agreement Activates Authority** When your words match God's Word, you step into spiritual authority and release heaven's power.

Journaling Questions

As you reflect on this chapter, journaling becomes a mirror to examine the power of your speech. What have you been saying? What patterns of declaration—or misdeclaration—have shaped your current emotional and spiritual landscape? By journaling these insights, you become more aware of how your words align with God's truth.

Use your journal to write your own declarations. Choose Scriptures that speak to your current season or struggle. Then personalize them. Turn them into present-tense affirmations of truth. This is not about pretending—it's about prophesying. You are declaring what God already says about you, allowing His Word to define your world.

Exposing My Vocabulary

What have I been saying about myself or my circumstances that doesn't align with God's Word?

_____
_____
_____
_____
_____
_____

Discovering Truth to Declare

What Scripture can I begin declaring to rebuild my thinking and speech?

_____
_____
_____
_____
_____

Building with My Voice

How can I make declaration a consistent part of my daily routine?

_____
_____
_____
_____
_____

Breaking Agreement with Lies

Are there specific lies I've been repeating aloud that I need to renounce?

_____
_____
_____
_____
_____
_____

Hearing Heaven's Language

What does heaven say about me that I've struggled to believe, and how can I begin declaring it?

_____
_____
_____
_____
_____
_____

Actionable Steps

Cultivate a List of Truths

Identify 5–10 Scriptures that speak to your identity, healing, and future. Write them out in your own words as declarations.

Equip Your Morning Routine

Begin each day by speaking your declarations out loud. Let your first words shape your mindset and spirit.

Engage in Ongoing Agreement

Anytime a negative thought or emotion arises, counter it immediately with a declaration. Make it your spiritual reflex.

Personal Reflection

Your voice carries the echo of your heart—and it also shapes the condition of your heart. What you say over yourself matters more than you know. Don't allow careless words to tear down what God is trying to build. Use your voice to speak life, build hope, and reinforce truth.

Declarations are more than positive thinking—they are prophetic alignment. When you declare God's Word, you're making a statement of faith that heaven recognizes. Keep going. Keep speaking. You're not just surviving—you're building.

What am I building with my words? Do my declarations agree with heaven or with fear? How different would my life look if I only spoke what God says about me?

Closing Prayer: *Father, thank You for giving me the power of words. I choose today to speak life, not death—to declare truth, not lies. Help me to use my voice to build, not break. Let every word from my mouth agree with Your Word. May my declarations shape my life to reflect Your heart. In Jesus' name, amen.*

Chapter 8

A Biblical Prayer for Wholehearted Healing

"Search me, O God, and know my heart; try me, and know my anxieties; and see if there is any wicked way in me, and lead me in the way everlasting." (Psalm 139:23-24, NKJV)

Some of the most life-changing moments in my healing journey came not through loud declarations or extended study, but through quiet prayers of surrender. I remember kneeling on the floor with my Bible open to Psalm 139, whispering the words, "Search me, O God." That prayer didn't come from a place of duty. It came from desperation. I wanted God to go deeper than I ever had before. I wanted Him to heal *all* of me—not just the parts I was comfortable surrendering.

That moment marked the beginning of a more vulnerable, honest walk with God. I stopped trying to manage my pain and started inviting Him into it. I realized that wholehearted healing only happens when I give God full access—not just to the wounds I can explain, but also to the ones buried beneath years of coping, defense mechanisms, and false identities.

Psalm 139 became more than a poetic passage—it became a personal prayer. Every line felt like a flashlight revealing what was in my heart. God wasn't exposing things to shame me. He was surfacing them to heal me. That's what biblical prayer for healing looks like: open-hearted, Spirit-led, and fully surrendered. It's not about praying perfectly—it's about praying honestly.

If you're ready for real healing, this kind of prayer is essential. You can't ask God to heal a heart you won't let Him see. But when you invite Him to search and lead you, He meets you with love, not condemnation. He guides you, gently but clearly, into wholeness.

Focus Point

"Search me, O God, and know my heart; try me, and know my anxieties... and lead me in the way everlasting." (Psalm 139:23-24, NKJV)

This scripture gives us a model for deep, healing prayer. It's not a list of requests—it's a posture of invitation. When we ask God to search our hearts, we're inviting Him to lead us beyond self-awareness into Spirit-revealed truth. This is where lasting healing begins—not through performance, but through presence.

Main Theme

The main theme of this chapter is the necessity of biblical, Spirit-led prayer in the process of healing. Prayers like the one in Psalm 139 are not casual or surface-level. They invite God to examine the core of who we are and reveal the things we often cannot see or articulate. These prayers do not originate from religious obligation but from a heart that desires transformation. When we allow the Holy Spirit to lead our prayers, He takes us to places in our heart that we've buried or avoided. But He doesn't stop there—He also leads us into freedom. This kind of prayer is the turning point in every healing journey.

> **"You can't be healed in the areas you won't pray about. Invite God into *everything*."**

Key Scriptures

- *"Search me, O God, and know my heart... and lead me in the way everlasting." (Psalm 139:23–24, NKJV)*
- *"The spirit of a man is the lamp of the Lord, searching all the inner depths of his heart." (Proverbs 20:27, NKJV)*
- *"Likewise the Spirit also helps in our weaknesses... the Spirit Himself makes intercession for us..." (Romans 8:26, NKJV)*

Key Points

- **Prayer Is a Doorway to Healing** Authentic prayer opens the heart and gives God access to the places that need healing most.

- **God Already Knows—But We Still Invite Him** Prayer isn't about informing God—it's about yielding to Him. He honors the invitation.
- **Healing Requires Vulnerability** Real prayer isn't polished. It's raw, honest, and willing to let God touch the deep places.
- **Spirit-Led Prayer Goes Deeper** When we pray under the Holy Spirit's guidance, we discover truths about ourselves we couldn't find alone.
- **You Don't Have to Know What to Pray** The Holy Spirit intercedes when we don't have the words. You just need to show up and surrender.
- **Prayer is the Place of Leading** God doesn't just search—He leads. His goal is always restoration and direction.
- **This Kind of Prayer Transforms You** Over time, prayers of surrender change your heart, habits, and emotional patterns.

Journaling Questions

This chapter is an invitation to deepen your prayer life beyond routine and into vulnerability. Journaling your prayers and insights gives form to what God is revealing in your heart. This process turns prayer into a dialogue rather than a monologue—it becomes a space of discovery, not just petition. Record what surfaces in prayer, especially as you pray Psalm 139 over yourself.

Use your journal as a place where you give God access. Don't just track what you're praying for—track what He is showing you. Write down the emotions, memories, and thoughts that rise up. Let your journaling be the record of your healing process—a testament to how prayer opened the door to inner transformation.

Invitation to Search

Am I truly open to God searching my heart? What do I fear He might find?

_____
_____
_____
_____
_____
_____
_____

Revealing the Hidden

What thoughts or emotions have I buried that God might be trying to surface for healing?

_____
_____
_____
_____
_____
_____

Letting the Spirit Lead

Am I allowing the Holy Spirit to guide my prayers, or am I trying to control the process?

_____
_____
_____
_____
_____
_____

Trusting God with the Deep Places

Where have I been hesitant to let God in fully? What would it look like to surrender those places?

_____
_____
_____
_____
_____
_____

Recognizing the Way Everlasting

What direction do I sense God leading me as I pray honestly and vulnerably?

_____
_____
_____
_____
_____
_____

Actionable Steps

Cultivate Surrendered Prayer Time
Set aside 10 minutes a day to pray Psalm 139:23–24 aloud and listen for the Spirit's response. Let it guide your prayer time.

Equip Your Journal with Honest Prayers
Begin writing your prayers like letters to God. Don't hold back—be raw, be real, and let the Holy Spirit lead.

Engage in Spirit-Led Listening
After each prayer, take time to sit in silence. Ask the Holy Spirit to speak or reveal an impression. Write down whatever He brings to mind.

Personal Reflection

There is no healing without honesty. And honesty begins in prayer. When you give God permission to search you, He always does it with gentleness, never shame. The invitation is not to be exposed—it's to be restored. This is the foundation of every wholehearted healing journey.

Don't fear what God might reveal. Fear staying wounded because you never asked. Prayer is where the healing begins, where walls come down and God's love enters fully. You can trust Him with your deepest places.

What am I still holding back from God? Where is He inviting me to pray more vulnerably? How would my heart shift if I let Him lead me fully into healing?

Closing Prayer: *Father, I invite You to search me, know me, and lead me. I trust that what You reveal, You also heal. Help me to surrender my whole heart to You—especially the parts I've hidden. Guide me into Your truth, into Your love, and into the way everlasting. In Jesus' name, amen.*

Chapter 9

The Evidence of a Healed Heart

"A good man out of the good treasure of his heart brings forth good; and an evil man out of the evil treasure of his heart brings forth evil. For out of the abundance of the heart his mouth speaks."
(Luke 6:45, NKJV)

Not long ago, someone asked me, "How do you know when your heart is truly healed?" That question stuck with me. I thought back on my own journey—how I used to respond to triggers, how I interpreted people's words or actions, how I treated others and even myself. What I realized is that the evidence of a healed heart isn't just in how we feel—it's in how we live, speak, and respond.

When my heart was still broken, I reacted out of fear, suspicion, and pain. But as God healed me, my default began to change. I found myself giving people the benefit of the doubt, offering grace, and speaking with kindness—even when it wasn't easy. It wasn't a forced behavior; it was the fruit of healing. My heart had changed, and so did my output.

Jesus said that what's in the heart eventually comes out through our words and actions. That means if we want to know the condition of our heart, we just have to observe our speech and responses. Are we quick to criticize or quick to bless? Do we assume the worst or extend the benefit of the doubt? These are more than personality traits—they are indicators of our heart's condition.

Healing isn't just internal—it has external evidence. It shows up in how we treat others, how we speak, and how we interpret life. If our hearts are truly whole, our lives will testify to it. And that's the kind of witness that brings glory to God.

Focus Point

"A good man out of the good treasure of his heart brings forth good... For out of the abundance of the heart his mouth speaks." (Luke 6:45, NKJV)

This verse makes it clear: our lives are shaped by our hearts. You can't fake what's in the core of you—it will eventually show. But when healing has truly taken place, your words become uplifting, your actions more compassionate, and your assumptions more grace-filled. Healing in the heart leads to transformation in the life.

Main Theme

The focus of this chapter is identifying the visible signs of inner healing. While healing begins as an internal process, it inevitably produces outward fruit. Jesus taught that the condition of the heart is revealed through the words we speak and the actions we take. If we've truly encountered God's healing, there will be clear markers—kindness, grace, emotional stability, and the ability to bless others from a genuine place. This chapter encourages us to evaluate our daily responses and see them not as random reactions, but as reflections of our heart's condition.

> **"A healed heart speaks life, sees with grace, and lives from love."**

Key Scriptures

- *"A good man out of the good treasure of his heart brings forth good... For out of the abundance of the heart his mouth speaks." (Luke 6:45, NKJV)*
- *"Create in me a clean heart, O God, and renew a steadfast spirit within me." (Psalm 51:10, NKJV)*
- *"But the fruit of the Spirit is love, joy, peace, longsuffering, kindness, goodness, faithfulness, gentleness, self-control." (Galatians 5:22–23, NKJV)*

Key Points

- **Words Reveal Healing** What you say without thinking is often the clearest evidence of whether your heart is healed or still hurting.

- **Responses Matter** Your first emotional or verbal reaction can show where your heart still needs healing or has been transformed.
- **Healing Produces Grace** When your heart is healed, you no longer need to protect yourself with blame, suspicion, or judgment—you respond with grace.
- **Fruit Follows Healing** Love, joy, peace, and self-control are not goals—they are fruit. If they're growing in you, healing has happened.
- **Forgiveness Is a Marker** The ability to release offenses and extend forgiveness is one of the strongest signs of a healed heart.
- **Compassion Becomes Natural** You begin to feel others' pain, not from your own wounds, but from a place of wholeness that desires to help.
- **You Interpret Life Differently** A healed heart doesn't assume the worst—it sees with new eyes, through the lens of love and hope.

Journaling Questions

This chapter calls you to become a fruit inspector in your own life. What do your words say about your heart? Are your reactions shaped more by pain or by peace? Journaling can help you trace patterns, highlight growth, and identify where God may still be at work.

Take time to reflect on recent conversations and reactions. What surfaced? Were they rooted in fear, insecurity, and bitterness—or in love, faith, and freedom? Your journal can become a tool for diagnosis and celebration. It will show you where healing has taken place and where it is still unfolding.

Examining My Words

What have my recent conversations revealed about the condition of my heart?

_____
_____
_____
_____
_____
_____
_____

Responding with Grace

How do I typically respond when I feel misunderstood, hurt, or challenged?

___

Measuring the Fruit

Do I see the fruit of the Spirit growing in my life? Which fruits are most evident—and which are lacking?

___

Releasing Offense

Is there someone I need to forgive as evidence of a healed and surrendered heart?

___

Seeing Through a Healed Lens

How have my perspectives shifted since beginning this healing journey?

_____
_____
_____
_____
_____
_____

Actionable Steps

Cultivate Self-Awareness
Pay attention to your daily speech. Write down anything that surprises you—whether life-giving or critical—and trace it back to your heart.

Equip with a Fruit Inventory
Once a week, do a "fruit check" using Galatians 5:22–23. Which fruit showed up? Which needs watering?

Engage Grace in Real-Time
When you're tempted to react in old ways, pause and ask: "What would a healed heart do right now?" Then do it.

Personal Reflection

A healed heart changes everything. It affects how you love, how you speak, and how you perceive the world around you. This chapter is not about striving to prove you're healed—it's about noticing the fruit that shows you are. Healing isn't hidden; it reveals itself in the most ordinary moments of your life.

As you continue this journey, let the evidence speak for itself. Don't just look for emotional relief—look for lasting transformation. Let your words be kinder, your assumptions softer, your grace deeper. That's what it means to walk in healing.

Am I living from a healed heart or still reacting from old wounds? What evidence of transformation do I see in my life? What would it look like to live fully healed, every day?

Closing Prayer: *Father, thank You for healing my heart. Thank You that my words and actions can reflect Your work in me. Help me to continue growing in grace, kindness, and truth. Let the fruit of healing show in my life—not to impress others, but to glorify You. In Jesus' name, amen.*

About the Author

Ben Díaz and his wife, Kara (author of Living the Abundant Life), are the founding pastors of Vida Church in Mesa, AZ. Ben began leading worship at the age of 15 at his parents' church in Mexico City, where he was born and resided until he became a missionary at 18. He then traveled across the US, Mexico, and Central and South

America, leading worship, translating, and directing Miracle Crusades. Ben and Kara founded Heaven on Earth Homes, an orphanage in Kenya. They have five kids of their own and many adopted

children in Africa.

Harrison House is a Spirit-filled, Word of Faith Christian publisher dedicated to spreading the message of faith, hope, and love through our wide range of inspiring publications. Committed to the messages that highlight the power of the Word and Spirit, we provide books, devotionals, and study guides that empower believers to live victorious, faith-filled lives.

Our resources are designed to help readers grow spiritually, strengthen their faith, and experience the transformative power of God's Word. Harrison House is passionate about equipping Christians with the tools they need to fulfill their divine purpose and impact the world for Christ.

www.ingramcontent.com/pod-product-compliance
Lightning Source LLC
Chambersburg PA
CBHW080839230426
43665CB00021B/2892